JEFF The

For Jamie Oliver
J. W.

For the Tzannes Family, Klub Barbounia members
K. P.

www.korkypaul.com

ORCHARD BOOKS
338 Euston Road, London NW1 3BH
Orchard Books Australia
Level 17/207 Kent Street, Sydney NSW 2000
ISBN 1 84362 146 0 (paperback)
First published in Great Britain in 2004
First paperback publication in 2005
A CIP catalogue record for this book is available
from the British Library.
1 3 5 7 9 10 8 6 4 2 (paperback)
Printed and bound in China
Orchard Books is a division of Hachette Children's Books

JEFF The Witch's Chef

Jeanne Willis * Korky Paul

ORCHARD BOOKS

JEFF

The Witch's Chef

Wotcha, mate. Be with you soon,
Just taste this soup, yeah? Lick the spoon.
I'll just bosh in a bit more salt -
And add a little splash of malt.

I love to cook stuff - it's my life.
I try out dishes on my wife.
There is no bigger thrill for me
Than thinking up a recipe.

I don't cook boring things, all right?
Let's say it's shepherds pie tonight.
I don't use minced-up lamb or beef,
No, I use real shepherds, chief!

I'm famous for gigantic pies.
I made one once - cor, what a size!
It took a ton of mammoth meat
And pastry bigger than a sheet.

Heavy? I should cocoa, mate.
I put it on a massive plate
And drove it up this beanstalk, like.
It really knackered up my bike.

The geezer there was pleased as punch.
Enormous bloke! He liked his lunch.
But when he saw my fee, fi-fum!
He wasn't very happy, chum.

I catered for this bloke, Jack Sprat.
His wife was really into fat.
I sorted them. It wasn't hard -
I steamed him leeks, I fried her lard.

I had a call to go to Norwich.
Was I any good at porridge?
I said I'd give the thing a stir.
(Completely bear, this trio were.)

They'd had a problem, so they said.
The little blonde girl in their bed
Complained the porridge was too hot,
And full of lumps. Oh dear, what?

"You don't want this old sticky glue,"
I said. "I'll tell you what I'll do,
I'll make a pukka fry-up, yeah?"
Which really pleased the daddy bear.

Baby bear was chuffed as nuts.
He stuffed his little furry guts
So much he couldn't zip his jeans.
Whoops! Pardon me. Too many beans.

One summer's day I made a tart.
Who was it for? A Queenie Heart.
Quite posh she was. She wore a crown,
Lived in a palace up the town.

I left it on her shelf, I swear.
I turned my back - it wasn't there!
She threw me out. Refused to pay
And said some Knave stole it away!

She had crumbs all down her cloak.
The Knave was innocent, poor bloke.
She ate that tart, all steaming hot
And scrumptious. Yeah, she scoffed the lot.

I am a wicked cook, it's true.
I can concoct a magic stew.
But mine is nourishing and rich,
Not like my client's, Mrs Witch.

I had a call from her last week.

"Come hither, Jeff." I heard her squeak.

"My children will not eat a thing,

They're thinner than a piece of string."

She told me to go round that night
To try and whet their appetite.
And give the fussy girl and boy
A supper they would both enjoy.

The witch lived in a spooky wood.
It did my moped wheels no good.
My baking tins fell off the back.
My chocolate chips fell down a crack.

A ghost nicked all my cooking spoons
(I heard it somewhere playing tunes).
My veg was pinched by a phantom horse.
A vampire stole my tomato sauce.

The witch was waiting by the gate.
I said, "I'm sorry that I'm late,
The ghosts and ghoulies nabbed my gear -
I'd watch it, luv, it's rough round here."

"Come and meet the kids," she said.
(Her house was made of gingerbread.)
"Feel free to use my cauldron, dear.
The weighing scales are over here."

I said, "They won't get very fat
On eye of newt and tongue of bat.
No, if you want those kids to eat,
Try treacle sponge or something sweet.

"They'll soon pile on the pounds," I said.
But while I buttered up the bread
I heard her whispering. She grinned,
"I'll have those little darlings skinned!"

She never realised I'd heard.
I didn't trust that mean, old bird.
I sent her out to fetch some sage
And found the children in a cage.

"Help us, famous chef!" they cried.
Poor Gretel sobbed, "We're stuck inside!
She'll have us roasted! Chopped in half!
Ooh...may I have your autograph?"

I'm a wizard, so they say,
At cooking, and I know my way
Around the kitchen, that is true.
My recipes are magic too.

I found a really weird book
About what witches like to cook
And secretly, I thought I'd make
The recipe for...Malkin Cake.

I searched the larder. There were lots
Of nasty things in little pots.
Toads in aspic, devilled flies,
And jars of pickled zombie eyes.

I cracked the eggs into my pot
And sneaked in everything I'd got;
The sun-dried slug, the dragon sneeze,
The marinaded ferret fleas.

I added syrup, nuts and spice
To make it all smell really nice,
Disguising I was up to tricks.
I baked the cake on gas mark six.

In half an hour, it was cooked
And very wonderful it looked.
I nearly cut myself a slice;
The witch said, "That smells really nice!"

She said, "It's far too good to waste
On kiddies! Let me have a taste."
She ate a mouthful. That was that!
She turned into a ginger cat.

"Fantastic!" Hansel cried, "We're free!"
I said I'd cook them both some tea.
"No way - your cooking sucks!" he said.
"We'll go to Pizza King instead."

Crazy Jobs

Written by Jeanne Willis * Illustrated by Korky Paul